Mythtery & Maynem

by Kim Esop Wylie

Commissioned by
The Repertory Theatre of St. Louis
Steven Woolf, Artistic Director
Mark D. Bernstein, Managing Director
Produced by The Imaginary Theatre Company and
originally entitled *Myth Adventures*

Single copies of plays are sold for reading purposes only. The copying or duplicating of a play, or any part of play, by hand or by any other process, is an infringement of the copyright. Such infringement will be vigorously prosecuted.

Baker's Plays
7611 Sunset Blvd.
Los Angeles, CA 90042
bakersplays.com

NOTICE

This book is offered for sale at the price quoted only on the understanding that, if any additional copies of the whole or any part are necessary for its production, such additional copies will be purchased. The attention of all purchasers is directed to the following: This work is protected under the copyright laws of the United States of America, in the British Empire, including the Dominion of Canada, and all other countries adhering to the Universal Copyright Convention. Violations of the Copyright Law are punishable by fine or imprisonment, or both. The copying or duplication of this work or any part of this work, by hand or by any process, is an infringement of the copyright and will be vigorously prosecuted.

This play may not be produced by amateurs or professionals for public or private performance without first submitting application for performing rights. Royalties are due on all performances whether for charity or gain, or whether admission is charged or not. Since performance of this play without the payment of the royalty fee renders anybody participating liable to severe penalties imposed by the law, anybody acting in this play should be sure, before doing so, that the royalty fee has been paid. Professional rights, reading rights, radio broadcasting, television and all mechanical rights, etc. are strictly reserved. Application for performing rights should be made directly to BAKER'S PLAYS.

No one shall commit or authorize any act or omission by which the copyright of, or the right to copyright, this play may be impaired. No one shall make any changes in this play for the purpose of production.

Publication of this play does not imply availability for performance. Both amateurs and professionals considering a production are strongly advised in their own interest to apply to Baker's Plays for written permission before starting rehearsals, advertising, or booking a theatre.

Whenever the play is produced, the author's name must be carried in all publicity, advertising and programs. Also, the following notice must appear on all printed programs, "Produced by special arrangement with Baker's Plays."

Licensing fees for *MYTHTERY & MAYHEM* is based on a per performance rate and payable one week in advance of the production.

Please consult the Baker's Plays website at www.bakersplays.com or our current print catalogue for up to date licensing fee information.

Copyright © 2008 by Kim Esop Wylie
Made in U.S.A.
All rights reserved.

MYTHTERY & MAYHEM
ISBN 978-0-87440-186-8
#1844-B

by Kim Esop Wylie
Directed by Kat Singleton

Scenic Design
Lou Bird

Costume Design
Betsy Krausnick

Stage Manager
Sarah Allison

Director of Education
Marsha Coplon

Artistic Supervisor
Jeffery Matthews

The Company

Pandora / **Meghan Brown**

Midas / **Jason Contini**

Persephone / **Maria Tholl**

Zeus / **Chauncy Thomas**

CHARACTERS

ZEUS: God of the gods
POSEIDON: God of the sea
HADES: Lonely and mostly silent God of death
HADES 2: same character as Hades, but played by a different actor
PROMETHEUS: Resourceful creator of man
EPIMETHEUS: Creator of Pandora – not the brightest god on Mt. Olympus
PANDORA: First human female – cursed from the get-go
SEED: Randy admirer of Persephone
DEMETER: Goddess of all plants and protective mother
PERSEPHONE: Loving daughter of Demeter
DIONYSIS: Dandy God of wine and song and something else he can't remember
KING MIDAS: Cursed by greed, but a loving father
SERVANT: Cockney serf who suffers at every turn
MIDAS' DAUGHTER: Young princess who loves her daddy
ECHO: Sweet nymph who is changed into a liar
NARCISSUS: Sweet, beleaguered cowboy-Shepard who becomes cruel
EROS: Little rascal God of love

FOUR PROFESSIONAL ACTOR COMBINATIONS

Actor: Zeus, Seed, Dionysus, Eros
Actor: Poseidon, Epimetheus, Hades 2, Midas, Narcissus
Actress: Narrator, Hades, Demeter, Pandora, Midas' Daughter
Actress: Prometheus, Persephone, Servant, Echo

For John Wylie

(Stage is empty. Ethereal music. Children's voices are heard.)

CHILD'S VOICE 1. Why are we here?

CHILD'S VOICE 2. Why is there winter?

CHILD'S VOICE 3. What happens when we die?

NARRATOR. *(enters)* For thousands of years, humans have pondered these questions. Three thousand years ago, the Greeks believed that many gods ruled the universe. In order to make sense of the world, the Greeks created stories – myths – about these gods, to explain love and hate, joy and sorrow, life and death. And winter. These are their stories. *(exits)*

(A loud crash of thunder. **ZEUS** *enters with a lightning bolt staff and holding an Earth ball.)*

ZEUS. Behold! The World!

(Another loud crash. **ZEUS** *laughs heartily.)*

ZEUS. I am Zeus! God of the Gods! I rule with my brother Poseidon, God of the Sea!

*(***POSEIDON*** "swims" in with a trident and exits.)*

Fine swimmer, that one. *(Announcing)* And my bother, Hades, God of the Underworld! King of the dead!

*(***HADES*** enters completely covered by a dark robe. We cannot see his face. He holds a scythe and exits.)*

Doesn't date much. *(back to big voice)* We are the Gods! And I am the Head God on Mount Olympus, the highest mountain in Greece! And we rule all! All of it! All the trees, and the water, and the… Who am I kidding? There's nothing here to rule! Just a bunch of plants. And liquid. We need some… creatures. Yes. That's it. Prometheus!

PROMETHEUS. Yes, Zeus, God of the Gods?

ZEUS. I'm bored. I want some creatures.

PROMETHEUS. Creatures?

ZEUS. *(indicating Earth)* You know, things to scurry around down there. And then we can play with them.

PROMETHEUS. Play?

ZEUS. Start wars, run races, love, hate, that sort of thing. Get right on it! *(ZEUS exits.)*

PROMETHEUS. Yes, sir, God of the Gods! *(salutes with dread)* Creatures? Oy! Epimetheus! Brother!

EPIMETHEUS. *(limps in)* Um, Yes, Prometheus?

PROMETHEUS. Zeus wants some creatures! Get right on it!

EPIMETHEUS. *(stupidly)* Creatures?

PROMETHEUS. You know… To scurry around on Earth. Fight wars, run races, love, hate. That sort of thing.

EPIMETHEUS. Huh?

PROMETHEUS. And give each one something special. So we can tell them apart. Zeus is waiting! *(exits)*

EPIMETHEUS. Okayyyy. Something special, something special.

(takes a blob of clay out of his tunic and tears off a hunk. Rolls it between his hands to make a long strip. Looks at it closely, until one end tries to bite him.)

Snake!

(laughs stupidly and rolls clay into a ball.)

Catch!

(tosses ball from one hand to the other, then drops clay.)

Oops.

(picks up clay, looking at its flat side. Moves it through the air.)

Turtle!

(rolls clay again into a ballish shape, then notices hands are dirty.)

Yuck.

(tries to wipe hands on self, but hands don't come clean. Spits on each hand, then is disgusted by the slobbery clay mess. Thinks.)

Fish!

(clay almost slides out of hands. Exits trying to hold on to it.)

(Music changes. **SEED** *somersaults onto stage, stops, rolled up into tight ball.* **DEMETER** *enters.)*

DEMETER. *(lovingly)* And what have we here? A seed? Wake up, sleepy head, wake up. I command you to grow!

(Music becomes faster, more upbeat. **SEED** *opens up and grows while sitting, then grows into standing.)*

PERSEPHONE. *(enters carrying a stone)* Mama! Mama, look what I found!

DEMETER. Oh, Persephone! It's beautiful!

PERSEPHONE. *(noticing* **SEED***)* Ohhh! Did you make that?

*(***DEMETER*** nods.)*

I wish I could be the goddess that makes everything grow!

DEMETER. You will be one day.

PERSEPHONE. I think you're even better and stronger than Zeus himself!

DEMETER. Hush, Persephone. We must not anger Zeus. All of us gods have our own special powers.

PERSEPHONE. Making things grow is the best power of all!

DEMETER. Come! Let's grow that field. You can choose the colors! *(exits)*

*(***PERSEPHONE*** starts to exit, then stops.)*

PERSEPHONE. Wait! My stone! *(looks around for it)*

*(***HADES 2*** enters, watches* **PERSEPHONE**. *Music of death is heard, but* **PERSEPHONE** *doesn't notice. As she exits skipping with her rock,* **HADES 2** *puts his arms out to her, disappointed that she is gone.)*

SEED. That Persephone. She's hot!

(**HADES 2** *waves his scythe at* **SEED**, *who slumps over, dead.* **SEED** *somersaults offstage.*)

PERSEPHONE. *(enters running)* Mama? Mama? *(looks to audience)* Flowers! They're the most beautiful ones I've ever seen! So many shapes and colors!

(**HADES** *looks around to make sure no one is there.* **HADES** *rushes at* **PERSEPHONE** *and grabs her. She screams as* **HADES** *drags her offstage.*)

DEMETER. *(enters singing)* Oh, Persephone, look at them! *(looking out at audience)* All different kinds, all together. Look at that flower! You can see its wisdom so clearly. And that one. Such spunk and spirit. And that one! So strong and kind. Persephone, do you think... Persephone? Are you hiding, dear child? Persephone? Come out. Come out! *(looks around, then to audience)* Flowers, you look sad. What is it? What's the matter? Oh, I forgot. You cannot speak. I command you to speak, dear flowers. Tell me why you look so troubled. I pray thee, speak! You, there! Flower in the blue jeans and red shirt! Tell me why you look so sad! *(waits for audience member to speak)* What? A dark figure, cloaked in... death? Hades, God of the Underworld! Took who? A girl? Persephone?! Oh! My daughter, taken to the realm of the dead! Only Zeus can save her! Thank you, flowers! Thank you! *(exits running)*

(*Music changes.*

EPIMETHEUS *enters with an armful of clay animals*)

EPIMETHEUS. *(sings off key)* Oh, I love my creatures so much! I'm singing a song about my creatures, 'cause I love them so much!

DIONYSIS. *(stumbles in hands over ears)* Killing! Murder!

EPIMETHEUS. *(worried)* Who's killing? What murder?

DIONYSIS. You! You're killing that music! Murdering that song! Cease!

EPIMETHEUS. Dionysis! You're drunk! Again!

DIONYSIS. As the god of wine and song, it's what I do.

EPIMETHEUS. *(singing loudly off key)* I don't like wine! I just like creatures! See my creatures? I made 'em myself! And they each have something special 'cause Prometheus told me to give each one something special, like turtles have flat bottoms –

DIONYSIS. *(yelling)* Silence, Music Killer!

EPIMETHEUS. *(angry)* I got creatures! Don't make me use 'em!

DIONYSIS. I've got... grapes! Don't make me use *them*!

(EPIMETHEUS takes some clay creatures and barks, growls, brays and howls at DIONYSIS, who uses his grapes in defense, but quickly gives up and stumbles offstage crying.)

PROMETHEUS. *(enters)* Epimetheus? Have you finished the creatures?

EPIMETHEUS. Uh, yep.

PROMETHEUS. I had an idea for one! Look! *(holds a clay human)*

EPIMETHEUS. *(circles, examining it)* What is it?

PROMETHEUS. Man!

EPIMETHEUS. What's man?

PROMETHEUS. It's for Zeus! See, it even looks like him! And he'll walk on two legs! And he'll be able to look up and worship all of us gods! And they'll be lots of them and they'll live on Earth. And with a brain big enough so that they don't try to eat rocks! *(EPIMETHEUS claps.)* But man needs a special gift. What about... wings?

EPIMETHEUS. *(holds up a bird)* Uh, I gave those to the birds. Tweet, tweet, tweet, tweet!

PROMETHEUS. What about... a tail? A big bushy man tail!

EPIMETHEUS. No more tails.

PROMETHEUS. What if we made man smell really, really bad?!

EPIMETHEUS. *(holds up the skunk)* Skunk.

PROMETHEUS. What else have you got?

EPIMETHEUS. I gave everything away! *(weeps stupidly)* No gifts for man!

PROMETHEUS. But man is the most special creature of all. Just as we are the gods of man, man will be gods of the creatures. He must have a special gift. The most special gift of all… *(getting an idea)* I know! Let's give man something… godly.

EPIMETHEUS. *(afraid)* Like what?

PROMETHEUS. Like… fire!

EPIMETHEUS. Zeus won't like it.

PROMETHEUS. Shhh! *(exits running)*

EPIMETHEUS. *(gathers clay figures)* Zeus won't like it! Zeus won't like it! Zeus won't like it! *(exits)*

*(Very loud snoring is heard. **PROMETHEUS** tip toes in carrying **ZEUS**'s lightning bolt.)*

PROMETHEUS. Zeus? Are you awake?

(Snoring gets louder.)

PROMETHEUS. Can I borrow a little, tiny piece of your lightning bolt?

(Loud snoring.)

PROMETHEUS. I'll take that as a yes! *(grabs an invisible piece from lighting bolt and exits running.)*

EPIMETHEUS. *(enters chanting)* Zeus won't like it. Zeus won't like it. Zeus won't –

*(**PROMETHEUS** enters running. They run into each other.)*

PROMETHEUS. Behold! Fire. And man.

(Loud thunder crashes.)

ZEUS. *(roaring offstage)* Prometheus!

EPIMETHEUS. Zeus doesn't like it, Zeus doesn't like it, Zeus doesn't like it! *(exits running)*

PROMETHEUS. Yikes! *(exits running but is stopped by Zeus, who holds Earth ball and lightning)*

ZEUS. Prometheus! What is this I see?

PROMETHEUS. *(whistles)* Beg your pardon, oh Great God of Everything?

ZEUS. This. On Earth. Something is… glowing!

PROMETHEUS. Maybe Apollo, the Sun God, dropped some, you know, sun. Or something.

(ZEUS shakes his head.)

PROMETHEUS. Ummm… Maybe it's a reflection! From a mirror!

ZEUS. I haven't invented mirrors yet.

PROMETHEUS. Oh.

ZEUS. *(angry)* It's fire! Where did man get fire?!

PROMETHEUS. It might have been… me.

ZEUS. *(very angry)* Only I possess fire! Whoever steals fire from me shall be chained to a rock and have his liver torn out of him for all eternity! Shazam!

(points lightning staff at **PROMETHEUS**, *who screams and spins offstage.)*

ZEUS. *(gazing at the Earth ball)* Man! You will pay dearly for using my fire! Shazam! *(starts to exit)*

*(***EPIMETHEUS*** enters with* **PANDORA** *who stands perfectly still.)*

EPIMETHEUS. Zeus, Oh Mighty God of… Mighty… Might! Looky what I made! Another creature!

ZEUS. Better not be anymore fire stealers – Oh my!

EPIMETHEUS. Yep.

ZEUS. *(whistles in appreciation)* I like it! What is it?

EPIMETHEUS. It's a… a… a woman.

ZEUS. What's that?

EPIMETHEUS. It's like Aphrodite, Goddess of Love –

(music of love plays. **ZEUS** *and* **EPIMETHEUS** *both look love struck for a moment)*

But human. And she'll live on Earth.

ZEUS. *(disappointed)* Oh.

EPIMETHEUS. With men!

ZEUS. Men? Men! Those ungrateful, conniving, fire stealing – *(gets an idea)* Oh. She's going to live with men, you say? What's her name?

EPIMETHEUS. You name her!

ZEUS. Let's call her… Pandora! Why, this calls for a celebration! And a gift! The most powerful gift of all. *(hands her a box)*

PANDORA. *(with difficulty speaking)* Thank you.

ZEUS. Oh, that's not my gift. This is my gift! I give thee… the gift of curiosity! Shazam! *(zaps her with staff)*

PANDORA. *(jolts wide-eyed, speaks quickly)* Curiosity? What's that? I've never heard of that. I wonder what that is? Does it hurt? Can I use it to clean my house? Can I eat it?

ZEUS. Enjoy! *(turns to leave)*

PANDORA. Wait! What's in the box? Is it a bug? Is it purple? Is it money? Ohmygosh, if it's money, can I spend it?

ZEUS. Pandora, my dear. Live long and well. But in return for my gift of curiosity, you must make me a promise.

PANDORA. A promise? I've never made a promise! What's the promise?

ZEUS. You must never open that box.

PANDORA. Oh. *(pause)* But I'm curious.

ZEUS. I know. *(exits laughing)*

EPIMETHEUS. Not good. Not good. Not good. *(exits)*

PANDORA. What do you think is in the box? I can't stop thinking about what's in the box. What do you think is in the box? I can't stop thinking about what's in the box. I know! I'll shake the box, and then I'll figure it out!

(shakes box delicately and frowns when she hears nothing. Shakes box slightly more. Nothing. Crazily shakes box, jumping up and down, grunting loudly. Stops, embarrassed. Then, losing all self-control)

WHAT IS IN THIS BOOOOOOOOX?!

(PANDORA flings herself and box around stage, screaming insanely.)

PANDORA. *(exhausted)* I can't stop thinking about what's in the box. I wonder what's in the box... *(wanders offstage still mumbling)*

PERSEPHONE. *(enters crying)* Please, Hades, God of the Dead! Please! You must let me go!

(HADES enters, walks by her.)

PERSEPHONE. Hades, without sunlight, without flowers, without my mother, I will die! Please let me go back up to Earth!

(HADES slowly shakes head)

PERSEPHONE. Please, I'll do anything! Anything! Just let me go.

(HADES holds out a hand.)

PERSEPHONE. What is it?

(HADES opens hand. PERSEPHONE looks at hand)

PERSEPHONE. Pomegranate seeds? I'm not hungry.

(HADES motions toward seeds and upward.)

PERSEPHONE. If I eat the seeds, I can go back up to earth?

(HADES nods)

PERSEPHONE. That's all?

(HADES nods.)

PERSEPHONE. So simple. Oh, I wish that my mother were here. She would help me. She would –

(HADES circles PERSEPHONE, slowly. Motions for her to follow. She starts to follow, then rushes back.)

PERSEPHONE. *(to audience)* Help me! I don't know what to do! Please! Help me!

(HADES 2 rushes to front row and aims scythe threateningly, slowly at audience, grabs PERSEPHONE, who struggles to get away, and exits.)

DEMETER. *(enters running)* Zeus! King of the Gods, I need your help! Persephone is gone!

ZEUS. *(enters)* Gone where?

DEMETER. The flowers told me she was taken by a dark figure!

ZEUS. You think it was –

DEMETER. Hades! He has stolen my daughter!

ZEUS. He hasn't had much luck with the lady gods.

DEMETER. I want her back NOW!

ZEUS. Demeter, if Hades has taken Persephone to the Underworld, there is not much I can do. That is his realm.

DEMETER. You are God of all gods! I am a goddess. Persephone is a goddess. I beg you, all powerful Zeus, rescue her!

ZEUS. I may not be able to bring her back.

DEMETER. You must!

ZEUS. If she has eaten any food of the Underworld, I cannot save her. You know that.

DEMETER. *(wildy)* Then all of earth shall die! Every tree, every grain. Every flower. Nothing will grow until Persephone is returned! *(exits)*

ZEUS. *(rolling his eyes)* Goddesses! Shazam! *(exits in a rage)*

(**HADES 2** enters, followed by **PERSEPHONE**)

PERSEPHONE. If I eat the seeds, you promise I can go back?

(**HADES** nods.)

You promise?

(**HADES** nods. **PERSEPHONE** takes the seeds, closes her eyes and eats them.)

ZEUS. *(enters, enraged)* STOP! Hades, you have stolen a goddess!

(**HADES** nods.)

ZEUS. She must return to earth.

(HADES *shakes head.*)

ZEUS. I command it!

(HADES *holds out seeds.*)

PERSEPHONE. Oh, great Zeus! Hades has promised to let me go if I ate these seeds! I'm coming with you!

ZEUS. *(pause)* No.

PERSEPHONE. But he told me –

ZEUS. He tricked you! Anyone who eats food of the underworld must stay – for all eternity.

PERSEPHONE. All eternity?

ZEUS. She must return. Her mother, Demeter, Goddess of the Harvest, has promised to kill every living thing!

(HADES *shakes head*)

ZEUS. By the Gods, you will free her!

(ZEUS *strikes at* HADES *with his lighting bolt.* HADES *blocks with scythe. They battle.*)

ZEUS. Enough! Persephone, how many seeds did you eat?

PERSEPHONE. *(miserably)* Six.

ZEUS. So shall it be! Six months you shall be here in the Underworld. And your mother's sadness will cause all of Earth to wither and die. Fall and winter.

PERSEPHONE. No! Please!

ZEUS. But then you shall return to your mother on Earth, and all the world will come to life again for six months. Spring. And summer.

PERSEPHONE. *(screaming)* Mother!

ZEUS. Be brave, Persephone. This is how it shall be. Forever more.

(HADES 2 *exits slowly, followed by the weeping* PERSEPHONE. ZEUS *exits opposite.*)

PANDORA. *(enters with box)* Must open box. Must open box. Can't open box!

(pushes it away from herself, but it crashes back to her)

I know! If I stop looking at it, maybe I'll stop thinking about it!

(sets box down and sits away from it. Looks at box, moves farther away. Looks at box again, moves farther away.)

I can't stop looking at it! Oh! I promised not to open the box. If only someone else could open the box!

(Sobs into her hands. One of her hands moves back and watches her. During the following, **PANDORA** *speaks for both herself and her hand.)*

HAND. Open it.

PANDORA. Who are you?

HAND. I'm your hand. And I say open the box!

PANDORA. Oh, I mustn't! Zeus made me promise!

HAND. Open it!

PANDORA. No!

HAND. Open it! Or else! *(hand becomes a fist)*

PANDORA. Help! Help! My hand is threatening me!

HAND. Open it, open it, open it!

PANDORA. Noooooo!

HAND. Then I'll open it!

PANDORA. Noooooo – *(pause)* Ok.

*(***PANDORA*** rushes to box, tears it open. Scary music, screams, and evil laughter echo loudly as dark, ragged words – GREED, CRUELTY, APATHY, and LIES – fly above* **PANDORA.***)*

PANDORA. *(cowering)* What are you?

VOICE 1. I'm Greed!

VOICE 2. I'm Cruelty!

VOICE 3. Apathy!

VOICE 4. Lies!

ALL VOICES. We will plague man – for all eternity!*(evil laughter)*

HAND. Close the box, close the box!

(**PANDORA** *rushes to close the box, but the evil shapes float away.* **PANDORA** *sinks to the ground.*)

PANDORA. What have I done? *(cries bitterly)*

QUIET VOICE. Hello?

PANDORA. *(looks around)* Who's there?

QUIET VOICE. In the box.

PANDORA. Oh, no! I'm not letting anything else out!

QUIET VOICE. But it's me. Hope.

PANDORA. Hope?

QUIET VOICE. You must let me out. The world needs me.

PANDORA. What are you?

QUIET VOICE. I am the only cure to greed, cruelty, apathy, and lies. When they strike, I will be there. I will strengthen the suffering. I will nurture the hurt. I will make it known that goodness is not lost.

PANDORA. Hope.

QUIET VOICE. You must let me go.

PANDORA. *(sadly)* You won't stay, though, will you?

QUIET VOICE. The world needs me.

(**PANDORA** *nods and slowly opens box.* **HOPE** *drifts from above.*)

PANDORA. Good bye, Hope. Now I am truly lost!

(*flops down and sobs loudly.* **HOPE** *hangs in the air.* **PANDORA** *looks up.*)

You're still here.

HOPE. I never leave those who need me.

PANDORA. But the world needs you.

HOPE. I can be everywhere. There is no limit to me.

PANDORA. Did Zeus put you in the box?

HOPE. Yes.

PANDORA. Then *you* are the most powerful gift of all. I promise never to lose you. Never.

(**HOPE** *floats gently offstage.* **PANDORA** *follows.*)

*(Music changes. **DIONYSIS** stumbles in, his arm around a large satyr doll.)*

DIONYSIS. And so Pandora lived a long, hope-filled life. She had many children. Pretty soon, there were humans everywhere. Like weeds. But, the evils from Pandora's box still plague man to this very day. Come, Silenus, let us sing a song about all of man's woes! I call it the Greed, Cruelty, Apathy and Lies song! *(sings)* Oh, Greed, Cruelty, Apathy and Lies – *(crying)* I hate greed, cruelty, apathy and lies!

(Mumbling is heard.)

DIONYSIS. You sleep while I sing?! I am Dionysis! God of wine and song and something else I can't remember right now. Why you... *(throws doll on the ground)* sleeping satyr, you! *(crying)* Sleeping while I'm singing! Hmph! *(stomps offstage)*

MIDAS. *(enters "riding" a hobby horse)* Smell that? That is my kingdom! I pride myself in a good smelling kingdom. *(sniffs again)* Whew. What's that? *(sees Silenus, sniffs him)* Sir! You are sleeping on the street! And you smell! Be gone! *(the doll doesn't move)* Be gone, I say! *(walks around doll)* I am King Midas and I command you to – It's a satyr! Everyone knows that satyrs are the special favorites of the god Dionysis. We must help the poor fellow! And then the gods will smile upon us! Servant!

*(claps. **SERVANT** enters)*

Take this poor satyr to my palace. And be careful. He must be a friend of Dionysis. Treat him as you would me. *(exits galloping)*

SERVANT. Poor lil' smelly bloke.

*(**SERVANT** delicately picks up doll. As she is bent over, **APATHY** floats from above with shrill laughter, and stings **SERVANT** in the rear. **APATHY** floats away.)*

SERVANT. OUCHIE MAMA!

*(**SERVANT** looks at satyr doll, then roughly throws doll on ground and exits kicking it.)*

DIONYSIS. *(stumbles in)* Silenus? Silenus! *(sings)* Oh, where oh where has my Silenus gone? Oh, where oh where can he be? With his ears like little pointy horns and his tail like a goat's, Oh where oh where can he be?

MIDAS. *(enters riding)* Not another smelly – *(stops in awe)* It's Dionysis!

DIONYSIS. Who are you?

MIDAS. Your loyal servant, Midas. King Midas.

DIONYSIS. *(crying)* Have you seen my satyr?

MIDAS. Yes, your Godship! He's at my palace.

DIONYSIS. You took him?! I'll… I'll turn you into a donkey!

MIDAS. I took him only to protect him, Oh Royal Stomper of Grapes!

DIONYSIS. Take me to him this minute! Or I'll turn you into a donkey with fleas!

MIDAS. Hop on! My stead will speed us there!

DIONYSIS. *(crying)* I'm afraid of horsies.

MIDAS. Oh, your royalness, horses are wonderful. Why, they're much like donkeys!

DIONYSIS. I hate donkeys! They have teeth, and eyes and ears!

MIDAS. You have teeth and eyes and ears.

DIONYSIS. *(throwing a tantrum)* Stop talking and take me to Silenus now!

MIDAS. This way, your Godliness!

*(**MIDAS** gallops out, followed by the wobbling "flying" **DIONYSIS**. **SERVANT** enters, still kicking doll. **MIDAS** gallops in.)*

MIDAS. Servant! Are you kicking that poor, helpless satyr?!

SERVANT. Whatever. *(exits)*

MIDAS. Can't get good help these days. *(to satyr doll)* Don't worry, little horned man. Your God friend will be here momentarily. Until then, I will care for you.

*(**GREED** descends along with scary music.)*

MIDAS. Hmm. Being the kind and gallant king that I am, I'd better check his breathing.

(bends over exaggeratedly. **GREED** *drifts down and pokes* **MIDAS** *in the rear end and exits amid shrill laughter.)*

OUCHIE MAMA!

DIONYSIS. *(enters)* Silenus! My satyr! You're safe! King Midas, I shall grant you one wish to honor your kindness. Even though you came dangerously close to being turned into a donkey.

MIDAS. Give me stuff! I want stuff!

DIONYSIS. What kind of stuff?

MIDAS. Gold stuff! Everything I touch, I want to turn to gold!

DIONYSIS. Good King, trust me. That's not a good idea.

MIDAS. *(chanting)* I want gold! I want gold!

DIONYSIS. So be it. Merlot! *(smacks* **MIDAS** *with his grapes.)* There. Now everything you touch shall turn to gold. You have my condolences. Come, Silenus. *(takes satyr doll and exits)*

MIDAS. Gold gold gold gold gold! *(dances around, staring at his hands. Laughs crazily, then sings to the tune of Soul Man)* I'm a gold man! Duh da da Duh da da! I'm a gold man! Play it, Steve! I'm a gold man... *(changes tune)* Happy gold day to me. Happy gold day to me! Happy gold day, happy gold day, happy gold day to... *(changes tune)* Me and my goldness, strolling down the avenue... *(exits dancing and screaming happily.)*

(Music change. **ECHO** *enters quietly)*

ECHO. *(whispers loudly)* Shhhhhh! We're playing my favorite game. Deer tickling! You have no idea how hard that is. Zeus and some nymphs are on the other side, and they're going to make the deer come this way, and when it jumps out, I get to tickle it! Oh, it's not mean. Deers love to be tickled. Shhh!

*(***ECHO*** bends over and peeks offstage.* **LIES** *floats down and stings* **ECHO** *in the rear.)*

ECHO. OUCHIE MAMA!

(**LIES** *floats away amid shrill laughter.*)

ECHO. *(yelling loudly)* Yaaaaaawwwww! That hurt!

ZEUS. *(enters)* Echo, shhhhhh! You scared the deer away!

ECHO. *(rubbing rear)* You did!

ZEUS. What?

ECHO. You scared it away! I saw it!

ZEUS. Echo!

ECHO. The deer saw you and was like, "I'm not going in there because that mean thunder pants Zeus is there and I totally hate him!" I heard the whole thing.

ZEUS. *(seething)* You lie, Echo!

ECHO. Sticks and stones may break my bones, but I heard that deer saying how much he hates you. And all the other gods hate you, too. They told me. So there.

ZEUS. No one lies to Zeus, God of the gods!

ECHO. The butterflies hate you, too. *(sticks out tongue)*

ZEUS. For being so careless with your words, Echo, I take them from you! Shazam! Forever more you shall only have the words of others! *(strikes her with lightning bolt and exits)*

ECHO. Words of others?!

(**ECHO** *tries to speak, but nothing comes out. She tries again. Nothing. She tries again. Nothing.* **ECHO** *sits down and cries silently.*)

NARCISSUS. *(enters running)* Hide me! *(tries to hide, then speaks to audience)* Have you seen a little cupid looking guy, yeah big, with a little bow and arrow? That's Eros, god of love. *(makes vomit noises)* He's the worst! Goes around shootin' people. Might look like a little nothin' of a weapon, but whoa dog, that thing is powerful! Like, I don't know what I ever did to that little dude, but he is after me! Every girl I meet, Eros shoots her with his arrow, and blammo! She's totally in love with me! It's a curse! *(winks at boy in audience)* You know what I'm talkin' 'bout, don't cha? Every girl is all over you, like, love, love, love! *(sees* **ECHO**, *whispers to audience)* Oh oh. A girl. Dern it. *(uncomfortably to* **ECHO***)* Um, excuse me, Miss. Have you seen Eros?

ECHO. Eros?

NARCISSUS. Little dude with a bow and arrow?

ECHO. Bow and arrow?

NARCISSUS. Phew! So you haven't seen him.

ECHO. Haven't seen him.

NARCISSUS. This might seem kind of forward and all, but I gotta ask you a personal question.

ECHO. A personal question?

NARCISSUS. You and me… you don't feel… I mean… there's no… love thang?

ECHO. No love thang.

NARCISSUS. Hot dog! In that case, it's nice to meet you! I'm Narcissus, the Shepard boy. Shepard man.

ECHO. Shepard man?

*(***EROS** *enters with bow and arrow.)*

EROS. Yo, Shepard Boy? Where'd he go? Oh, Narcissus! I got a little present for you! *(laughs nasally)*

NARCISSUS. Hide!

ECHO. Hide!

EROS. *(rapping)*
My name is Eros
Little god of love
Sent down from Olympus
Like a gift from above

I got me an arrow
And I got me a bow
I shoot you in the heart
And watch your love grow

I'm bad and I'm funny
Don't mess with me
Or I'll make you fall in love

With the next thing you see!

(laughs nasally) Haaaaaaaaa! *(aims arrow)* Doiing!

NARCISSUS. *(running)* Run away!

ECHO. *(running)* Run away!

(**NARCISSUS** *and* **ECHO** *run crazily.* **EROS** *chases them, trying to get a good shot.* **NARCISSUS** *and* **ECHO** *exit running.*)

EROS. You can run, but you can't hide! *(laughs nasally and shoots arrow offstage.)* Doiing! Oh oh. Missed him again! *(exits)*

(**ECHO** *stumbles back on stage, an arrow sticking out of her chest.* **NARCISSUS** *enters.*)

NARCISSUS. Oh, dude! He gotcha!

ECHO. Gotcha. *(stares stupidly in love at* **NARCISSUS***)*

NARCISSUS. Oh, dern it all! Now, you love me!

ECHO. Love me!

NARCISSUS. I'm sorry I gotcha in this here mess!

ECHO. *(happily)* This here mess.

NARCISSUS. Now what am I gonna do?

ECHO. *(naughtily)* What am I gonna do?

(**CRUELTY** *floats down and stings* **NARCISSUS** *in the rear and floats away.*)

NARCISSUS. OUCHIE MAMA!

ECHO. *(surprised)* Mama!

NARCISSUS. *(now cruel)* I ain't your mama!

ECHO. *(drunk with love)* Your mama!

NARCISSUS. And you ain't my mama!

ECHO. My mama!

NARCISSUS. You ain't your mama!

ECHO. Your mama!

NARCISSUS. Listen, knucklehead. You ain't your mama and you ain't my mama. So who are you?

ECHO. You!

NARCISSUS. You ain't me, dunce!

ECHO. Dunce!

NARCISSUS. *(starts to exit)* I'm leavin'.

ECHO. *(follows)* Leavin'!

NARCISSUS. *(running)* Don't follow me!

ECHO. *(running)* Follow me!

NARCISSUS. No way!

ECHO. Way!

NARCISSUS. Stop!

ECHO. Stop!

NARCISSUS. You stop!

ECHO. You stop!

NARCISSUS. *(stops)* Don't! Just... leave! *(exits)*

ECHO. Don't just leave! *(follows him offstage)*

(MIDAS' DAUGHTER enters singing, holding a doll. DIONYSIS enters opposite with branches sticking out of his clothes and hair.)

MIDAS' DAUGHTER. La la la. What happened to you?

DIONYSIS. A tree.

MIDAS' DAUGHTER. Phew! You smell!

DIONYSIS. I'm Dionysis! God of wine and song and... something else I can't remember right now.

MIDAS' DAUGHTER. Drinking makes you throw up.

DIONYSIS. *(crying)* Yes, it does.

MIDAS' DAUGHTER. I don't like throwing up! I'm a princess!

DIONYSIS. *(crying)* I don't like throwing up. And I'm a god!

MIDAS' DAUGHTER. *(hands his a handkerchief)* Here.

DIONYSIS. *(blows nose nosily)* Thank you. Are you really a princess?

MIDAS' DAUGHTER. You betcha!

(A horrible, multi-voiced scream.)

MIDAS' DAUGHTER. *(frightened)* What's that?

DIONYSIS. Pan. He must be angry.

MIDAS' DAUGHTER. Pan?

DIONYSIS. The god of nature. When he's angry –

SERVANT. *(enters running; almost incoherent)* Pan! Ick! Pan! Ick! Pan! Ick! Pan ick! Pan-ick! Panic! Panic! Panic! Aughhghghghghhghh! *(exits running)*

MIDAS' DAUGHTER. What's panic?

DIONYSIS. That.

MIDAS' DAUGHTER. I think that was my father's servant.

DIONYSIS. Your father's… ?

MIDAS' DAUGHTER. King Midas!

DIONYSIS. Oh, dear.

MIDAS' DAUGHTER. What's wrong?

DIONYSIS. Oh, dear dear dear dear dear.

MIDAS' DAUGHTER. Why do you say oh dear dear dear dear dear?

DIONYSIS. Young Princess. Your father has been bitten by –

MIDAS' DAUGHTER. A snake? *(**DIONYSIS** shakes head)* A spider? *(**DIONYSIS** shakes head)* A shark?!

DIONYSIS. Greed.

MIDAS' DAUGHTER. Greed? *(**DIONYSIS** nods)* What's greed?

MIDAS. *(enters running)* Gold! Gold! Gold! *(laughs maniacally)* Mine! Mine! Mine! *(more maniacal laughter)*

DIONYSIS. That is greed. Run! *("flies" wobbly offstage)*

MIDAS. Money, money, money! Gold and money! Money and gold! Gold and stuff! Gold stuff! Ha ha ha!

MIDAS' DAUGHTER. Daddy?

MIDAS. Daughter!

*(**MIDAS' DAUGHTER** stretches out her arms, still holding doll. **MIDAS** runs toward her, snatches doll, turns quickly. Doll is now gold.)*

MIDAS. Viola! I'm the man! The gold man!

MIDAS' DAUGHTER. Miss Betsy! *(snatches doll away from **MIDAS**, then falls to the ground with the doll's weight)*

MIDAS. *(singing and dancing)* I am the gold man, I am the gold man, la la la la la, I am the gold man!

MIDAS' DAUGHTER. Daddy! I can't move her!

MIDAS. *(claps)* Servant!

SERVANT. *(enters still twitching)* Yes, sire?

MIDAS. Move my daughter's doll!

(**SERVANT** *tries to pick up doll but can't*)

MIDAS' DAUGHTER. I hate gold!

MIDAS. *(shrieks in shock)* Whhhaaa?

MIDAS' DAUGHTER. Turn her back, Daddy! Turn her back!

MIDAS. But it's gold! Gold!

MIDAS' DAUGHTER. *(crying)* I want Miss Betsy back!

MIDAS. But see how happy she looks? *(all look quizzically at doll)* Miss Betsy likes being gold, don't you Miss Betsy? *(pretends to be voice of Miss Betsy)* Oh, yes, your highness! I love being gold! Gold, gold, gold *(turns back into evil greedy* **MIDAS** *voice)* gold, gold, gold!

MIDAS' DAUGHTER. *(crying)* Daddy!

MIDAS. Whew! All this gold making has made me hungry. Servant! Bring me some food!

SERVANT. *(enters running with a bowl of fruit)* Panic.

MIDAS. Yes! Food! *(picks a piece of fruit, then yells and spins at the same time)* Eureka! It's gold! *(singing)* I am the gold fruit man, I am the gold fruit man!

SERVANT. *(exits twitching)* Panic.

MIDAS. I'm the most golden, wonderful, magical king that ever was! *(tries to bite the fruit but can't. Tries again, but can't. Tries again.)*

MIDAS' DAUGHTER. Duh, Daddy. It's gold.

MIDAS. *(happily)* Yes, it is! My fruit is gold! My fruit is... *(stops)* But I'm hungry. I'm...

MIDAS' DAUGHTER. *(in horror)* Daddy... Will all your food turn to gold?

MIDAS. Of course not, Daughter! Why, I could just eat without touching anything! Not to worry!

MIDAS' DAUGHTER. But your teeth would touch it?

MIDAS. *(thinking)* Then I'll have the servant blend

everything, and I'll just drink my food through a straw!

MIDAS' DAUGHTER. What about your tongue?

MIDAS. My tongue? My… *(bursts into tears)* What have I done?! I'll starve! Everything I eat or drink will turn to gold!

MIDAS' DAUGHTER. *(wailing)* You're gonna die!

MIDAS. *(wailing)* Oh, what a curse! How could I have been so foolish!

MIDAS' DAUGHTER. Daddy! *(runs to him, embraces him, and freezes)*

MIDAS. *(screams)* Daughter! Daughter! *(tries to pry her off, but she is frozen in her embrace)* MY DAUGHTER! HELP! HELP! *(drags her offstage)*

*(Music change. **EROS** runs in.)*

EROS. Where'd he go, where'd he go? Narcissus is going down! Need a trap, need a trap… I know! *(pulls out a blue matt and throws it down.)* Hahahaha! A lake! Doiing! *(hides)*

*(**ECHO**, still with arrow sticking out, enters exhausted. Sees lake, stumbles to it, and drinks from it, which is difficult with the arrow. She stands, tries to pull out arrow. Tries again. Tries again and falls down.)*

EROS. Oh no! She's dead!

ECHO. *(sits up suddenly)* Dead?!

EROS. Echo! I didn't mean to shoot you. I was aiming for Narcissus! I've been after him for years!

ECHO. *(dreamy)* After him for years.

EROS. Not that way. He's supposed to fall in love. But he won't fall in love unless I shoot him.

*(**NARCISSUS** enters, exhausted.)*

ECHO. Shoot him!

EROS. *(aims at **NARCISSUS**)* Say cheese!

NARCISSUS. Dern it!

(ECHO and EROS both chase NARCISSUS. NARCISSUS yells at ECHO)

Stop chasing me, you, you, cow! You're a pest, and a vermit, and a yellow-bellied she-dragon who can't say nothing 'cept what anybody else says! I don't ever want to look at your dirty rotten repeatin' face ever again!

ECHO. *(extremely hurt)* Ever again?

NARCISSUS. Ever!

EROS. Narcissus! You're gonna be sorry for that!

ECHO. *(drifting backward)* Sorry for that. Sorry for that... Sorry for that... *(exits)*

EROS. You broke Echo's heart, you, you... Heart breaker! Yaaaaaa!

(chases NARCISSUS again. NARCISSUS runs offstage. EROS aims and shoots offstage. NARCISSUS yelps.)

Got him! Take that, Mr. Shepard Man! I hope the first thing you see is a spider! Or a worm! Or a skunk! That'll teach you to be cruel to someone who loves you! Doiing! *(exits)*

(NARCISSUS stumbles on stage with an arrow sticking out of chest. He careens around stage, mumbling and whining. At last he falls by the lake.)

NARCISSUS. Water.

(He drinks from the lake, and stops when he sees his reflection. He is suddenly filled with strength and passion.)

EROS. *(enters)* And another thing –

NARCISSUS. *(to lake)* Hello, good lookin'! What's a nice, purty face like you doing in a lake like this? Dern it. I think... I think I love you! Why, yes, I do! Would you, would you marry me? Yes, indeed, we ought to get hitched. I'll go git the preacher. *(moves back)* Where'd you go? Where'd you... ?

(looks into lake again) Hello, good lookin'! I guess I'll just stay here, then. And just look at choo. And your

purty face.

EROS. Worse than a skunk! He fell in love with… himself!

NARCISSUS. *(to his reflection)* What'cha thinkin' 'bout?

EROS. *(disgusted)* Loving yourself too much! That's just…

NARCISSUS. *(dabs lake)* Tickle, tickle, tickle!

EROS. *(gets an idea)* Narcissistic! Oy! What have I done?! I'll be the laughing stock of Mount Olympus!

(**NARCISSUS** *kisses lake*)

EROS. Hey! Stop makin' out with yourself!

(**NARCISSUS** *doesn't stop.*)

EROS. Stop kissing yourself! Right now! I'm going to give you to the count of ten! One!

(**NARCISSUS** *continues to kiss lake.*)

Two!

(**NARCISSUS** *continues to kiss lake.*)

Ten! Doiing*!*

(points arrow at **NARCISSUS**, *who sits up and with the flip of fabric, is transformed into a Narcissus flower.)*

A little yellow cup,
A little yellow frill,
Narcissus loved himself too much
Now he's a daffodil!
Doiing!

(Drags **NARCISSUS** *offstage. Music changes.* **SERVANT** *rolls in* **MIDAS' DAUGHTER**, *who sits frozen on a dolly. Takes out a feather duster and dusts her. Stops. Snaps fingers in front of her face. Wiggles fingers. Steps back and jumps in front of* **DAUGHTER**, *dancing and yelling gibberish, trying in vain to get a response.* **MIDAS** *enters wailing, stops.)*

MIDAS. What are you doing?

SERVANT. *(dusting* **DAUGHTER** *again)* Dusting.

MIDAS. *(wailing)* Were you… speaking gibberish to my daughter?!

SERVANT. No, Your Highness.

MIDAS. *(distraught)* I'll have no gibberish spoken to my daughter! Do you understand?!

SERVANT. No gibberish, Your Highness!

MIDAS. And none of this, either! *(waves and snaps fingers)*

SERVANT. No, Sire!

MIDAS. Or this! *(dances like **SERVANT**)*

SERVANT. *(starts to cry)* No, Your… Royal… Hi – *(dissolves into tears)*

MIDAS. *(wailing)* That you can do.

SERVANT. *(sobbing)* Thank you.

MIDAS. *(wailing)* I miss her!

SERVANT. *(wailing)* I don't like dusting her!

*(Both sob loudly. Music change. **HOPE** floats down from above. Both slowly stop crying.)*

MIDAS. Maybe someday she'll wake up.

SERVANT. Maybe someday you'll hire somebody else to dust her!

MIDAS. Maybe we'll run and play like we used to.

SERVANT. Maybe I could get me own servant!

MIDAS. Maybe someone could help us.

SERVANT. We could ask the gods?

MIDAS. Ask the gods for help! Why, that's genius! Sheer genius! Which gods?

SERVANT. Well, Sire, I'm only a servant with a teeny little servant brain, but how about Dionysis?

MIDAS. Yee gads! That's it! Then maybe… Maybe there's still… *(sees **HOPE** and points to it.)*

SERVANT. Can't read, Sire.

MIDAS. It says "hope."

SERVANT. Oh! I thought it said No Parking.

MIDAS. Hope!

SERVANT. Hope is much nicer than No Parking!

*(**MIDAS** and **SERVANT** jump up and down with*

excitement chanting "HOPE.")

MIDAS. Dionysis! Dionysis! Please help us!
DIONYSIS. *(stumbles in)* What now?!
SERVANT. That was easy!
MIDAS. My daughter! She's –
DIONYSIS. Gold. Isn't that what you wanted?
MIDAS. Not my daughter! Look at her! She's –
DIONYSIS. Dead. Killed by greed. Your greed. *(crying)* I tried to warn you...
MIDAS. *(crying)* Please! I'll do anything! Let my daughter live!
SERVANT. *(crying)* Please turn her back! It takes two hours to dust her!
DIONYSIS. *(crying)* Does anyone have a handkerchief? *(no one does)* Your daughter gave me a handkerchief. (**ALL** *cry harder)* I shall turn your daughter back! But there is a price, Midas.
MIDAS. Anything! I'll pay anything!
SERVANT. He'll give you his whole kingdom!

(Both stare at her)

MIDAS. I would do anything to have my daughter back! Anything!
DIONYSIS. I will change your daughter. And I will also take back the golden touch.
SERVANT. I knew you was a good bloke, even if you do stink!
MIDAS. Please, Dionysis, take it away! It's a curse.
DIONYSIS. In return, you shall change! You shall be what greed has made you! *(giggles and prances stupidly)*
MIDAS. Be what greed has made me?
SERVANT. You mean he'll be an idiot?
DIONYSIS. Do you agree to the terms? Oh, say yes! Say yes!
MIDAS. Anything! Just bring her back!
DIONYSIS. Cabernet! *(smacks* **MIDAS** *with grapes)*

MIDAS' DAUGHTER. *(waking)* Daddy?

MIDAS. Daughter?

MIDAS' DAUGHTER. Daddy!

MIDAS. *(embracing* **DAUGHTER***)* Thank you, Dionysis! Thank you!

SERVANT. Woo Hooo! *(throws feather duster over backdrop)*

DIONYSIS. *(giddy)* When you wake tomorrow, you will be what you were. Fare well! *(exits skipping)*

MIDAS' DAUGHTER. Bye, Mr. God of Wine!

MIDAS. I shall ever be in your debt, oh great Dionysis!

MIDAS' DAUGHTER. What did he mean about tomorrow? "You will be what you were"?

MIDAS. I don't know, sweetheart.

MIDAS' DAUGHTER. *(disgusted)* You're not going to turn into gold, are you, Daddy?

MIDAS. *(laughing)* I hope not, my dearest. I hope not.

SERVANT. Off to bed with you, missy. You've had a long day being a precious metal. *(steers* **DAUGHTER** *offstage)*

(Music. Moon comes up over backdrop and goes down. Sun comes up. A cock crows. **MIDAS' DAUGHTER** *enters sleepily and yawns.* **MIDAS** *enters opposite and yawns. He has donkey ears.)*

MIDAS' DAUGHTER. Morning, Daddy.

MIDAS. Morning, Daughter.

(They walk by each other. **DAUGHTER** *stops, does a double take at* **MIDAS***' ears.)*

MIDAS' DAUGHTER. You are what you were!

MIDAS. What, Sweetheart?

MIDAS' DAUGHTER. *(doubles over with laughter)* I get it!

MIDAS. Get what?

MIDAS' DAUGHTER. You! Your ears!

MIDAS. *(touching ears)* My ears? You mean, when I was greedy, I was –

MIDAS' DAUGHTER. Oh, that Mr. Dionysis is some funny god!

MIDAS. *(yelling)* Dionysis!

MIDAS' DAUGHTER. What's the matter, Daddy?

MIDAS. *(starts to cry)* I don't want to be a donkey.

MIDAS' DAUGHTER. Oh, but Daddy. The "gold, gold, gold" scared me. I like you this way.

MIDAS. *(after a moment)* If you like me this way, then so do I.

MIDAS' DAUGHTER. Then let's play! I'll be the princess and you be the donkey king! All hail King Donkey! Wait! You need some braids for your ears! Pink ones! With glitter! *(races offstage)*

MIDAS. *(looks up)* Thank you, Dionysis. Thank you, gods. *(pauses with the realization)* I have the most golden treasure of all. *(looks offstage after **DAUGHTER** and exits)*

(Music change)

ZEUS. *(enters with lightening staff and earth)* Behold! The World!

CHILD'S VOICE 1. Why are we here?

*(**PROMETHEUS** enters with clay man.)*

CHILD'S VOICE 2. Why is there winter?

*(**DEMETER** enters.)*

CHILD'S VOICE 3. What happens when we die?

*(**HADES 2** enters with scythe.)*

ZEUS. We are the gods! And we rule all! All of it! All the trees and the water. *(pauses, looks around at audience)* And the humans. And the... *(looks up)* Kind of empty up there. We need something...

*(**PROMETHEUS**, **HADES 2**, and **DEMETER** look at each other, whisper to each other, then step forward and whisper to **ZEUS**.)*

Yes! Yes! That's it! Shazam!

*(**ZEUS** waves lightening bolt. Constellations appear above the backdrop.)*

ZEUS. We are the Gods!

The End

PROPS

Character	Prop	Notes
Zeus	Lightening Staff	With detachable lightening bolt
Zeus	Earth Ball	Inflatable Beach ball
	Poseidon cut out	Drawing on 4' stick
Hades	Scythe	Has to do stage combat with Zeus
Prometheus	Clay	Crayola Foam clay
Persephone	Stone	
Epimetheus	Clay animals	Including a bird and a skunk
Dionysius	Gold Goblet	
Epimetheus	Clay Man	10-12" like animals
Pandora	Gold Treasure box	Needs to hold scarves Same as A&G
	Pedestal	Same as A&G
Hades	Pomegranate Seeds	
Pandora	Scarves	Colored Chiffon Tied together on Fishing Line. All but hope. 24" x 12"
	Scarves on Poles	Colored Chiffon With Printed Words " Hope (White), Greed (Green), cruelty(Red), apathy (Light Blue), lies (lavendar) Poles approximately 4'
	Satyr Doll	Approx 4' Needs to take a beating
Midas	Hobby Horse	
Eros	Bow and arrows	Some arrows will Velcro to costume
Midas's Daughter	Flip Doll	One side gold
Servant	Gold Fruit	
Servant	Fruit and Fruit Bowl	
	Water	Blue china silk about 6' long comes through wall
	Stool	Same as A&G
	Bench	Wooden Type bench
	Feather Duster	
	Constellations on sticks	Approx 2'

Also by
Kim Esop Wylie

Aesop's (Oh So Slightly) Updated Fables

The Bremen Town Musicians
The Dullsville Mystery
Fit
More Aesop's ...Updated Fables
Spirator City

Please consult the
Baker's Plays Catalogue
for complete details or find us online at
www.bakersplays.com

www.ingramcontent.com/pod-product-compliance
Lightning Source LLC
Chambersburg PA
CBHW071847290426
44109CB00017B/1957